by Piera Paltro

Hail Mary

TRANSLATED BY
DAUGHTERS OF ST. PAUL

ILLUSTRATIONS BY
ANNA MARIA CURTI

BOOKS & MEDIA
Boston

HAIL MARY, full of grace

I like
to call you by name
and say to you, "Hail!"
In your days the people
used to greet each other
that way.
And I also say to you,
"Full of grace."
Mary, full of grace,
means
that God made you
so good,
Immaculate,
without even
the tiniest sin.

It is wonderful
to know
that you have
an all-pure heart!
And our Father, God,
loved you so much
that He made you
the Mother
of His Son
Jesus.
Your friends
try hard
not to hurt you
by sinning.
I will try not to sin,
Mary.
To remind myself, I will
say often,

**HAIL MARY,
full of grace,**

the Lord is with you

You lived
in a beautiful little town
in the Holy Land,
and certainly you loved
flowers, birds,
and children.
Your friends used to
come and visit you.
But I know that God, too,
always came to visit you;
in fact, He lived right
in your heart,
because you were
so good.
And you liked to be
with Him
more than with
anyone else.

I would like to remember more
often that God lives in me, too,
as in His own house.
I like to stay with Mom
and Dad and with my friends
and also with my dog
when he wants to play.
But I could be a little more
thoughtful
toward the good God
who lives in my heart!
Please, Mary, remind me
that He is also always with me
every time I say to you,

the Lord is with you.

Blessed are you among women

I know that there are
many famous women.
There are queens,
movie actresses
and some who are even
police chiefs.
I do not know, Mary,
if in your times
you were famous.
Perhaps the king then
did not know you,
and yet you are
God's Mother.
Because you are God's Mother,
you became the most famous
of all women.

You were not rich;
you did not have any servants.
But you trusted in God,
and you loved Him so much
that He chose you to be His mother.
And now you are queen
of heaven and earth,
but you command only good things,
and you ask them of Jesus,
who never tells you "no."
No other woman
is as important as you!
I really mean it
when I say to you:

**blessed are you
among women.**

and blessed is the fruit of your womb, Jesus

We had a big party once
for the Baptism
of a baby just born.
There was candy,
there were friends
and everyone was happy.
When a new baby
comes into the world,
there is a party.
But what a gift
for everyone
when your Jesus
was born!

He was
happy, healthy and the
best child
in all the world.
How many times
your friends told you,
"How beautiful your
baby is,
Mary!"

How happy you were when
you thought
to yourself
that He was the Son
of God,
the God of the
whole world.
If they would have
known it,
they, too, would have
said with me,

and blessed
is the fruit
of your womb,
Jesus.

Holy Mary, Mother of God

I know who Saint Rita is
and also Saint Therese
and Saint Maria Goretti.
There are many women saints.
But you are much greater
than all of them.
To you, God Himself,
who made the whole world,
said,
"Hello, Mommy."
"Mother, may I do this?"
You are the most
important mother!

Who knows
how surprised you were
when the angel
came to tell you
that God
wanted to make you
mother of His Son!
I like to think about
how God, too,
chose to have a mother!
So I say to you,

**Holy Mary,
Mother of God...**

pray for us sinners

When my shoes are untied
or my face is dirty,
Mother says to me,
"Come here,"
and she helps me.
You, Mary full of grace,
are also our mother,
because Jesus
is our brother,
and so you, too,
look at us to see
if we are all right.

But, Mother Mary,
you see in my heart
what even my mother
does not see.
And you are displeased
when you see
that I have done something bad.
And then you say to Jesus:
"Help these little ones
to do better."
It is a good thing that you
think of this.
Do it always,
because it is not easy to
always do what is right!
With my whole heart
I say,

pray for us sinners...

...now

You know, Mother Mary,
I do not always behave
as well as I should.
In the morning when it is
time to get up,
at night before I fall asleep,
and at other times, too,
if I want,
I can act right, but
I can also do wrong things.

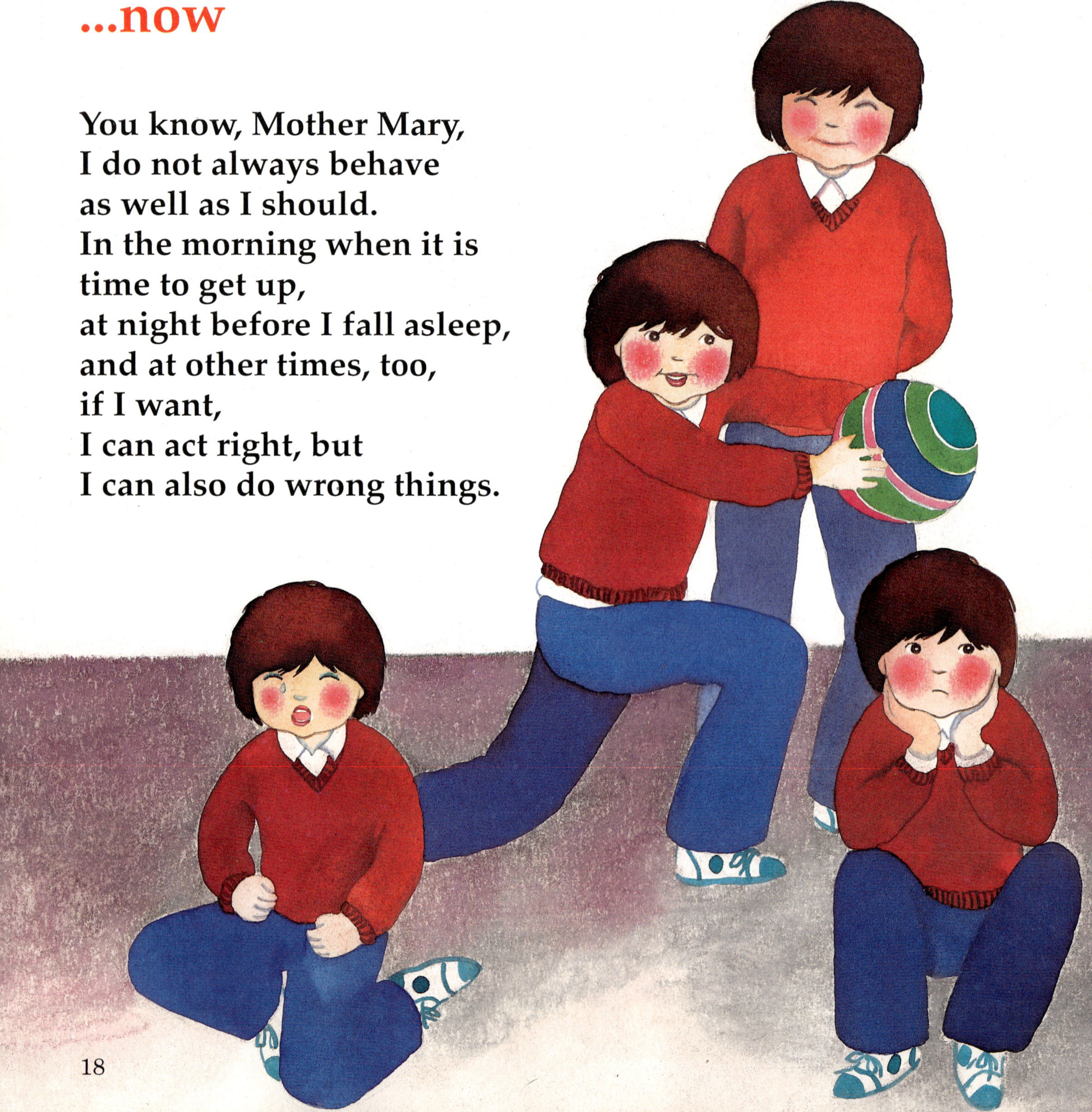

Please tell Jesus
to help me always,
even when I am
grown up,
until the end of my life.
NOW means: today,
tomorrow, and after tomorrow.
Now means ALWAYS.
I will try to remember this
when something is hard for me.
Then, I will say to you softly, softly,
Mother Mary, help me, help me

now...

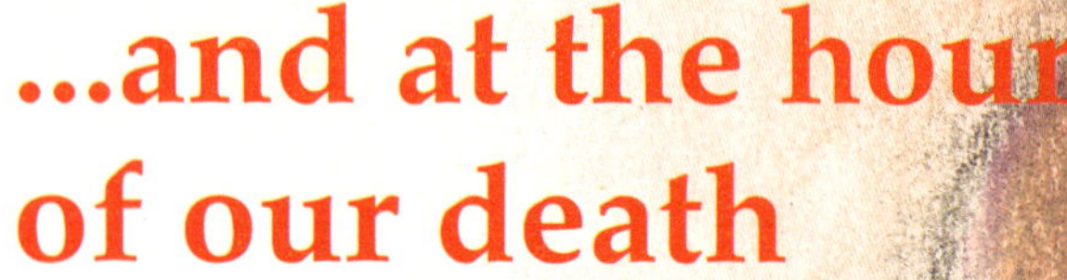

...and at the hour of our death

How strange.
Each of us knows when
he or she was born,
and none of us knows
when he or she will die.
When we die,
we will meet Jesus.
He will ask us if
we have tried our best
to please Him.
We want
to be able to answer
"yes."

You, Mother Mary,
watched very sadly
while Jesus died
on the cross.
You heard when He said
to the thief
near Him
that He forgave him
and would meet him in
heaven.
We understand
that when we die
you are very, very close
to help us go
to Jesus!
And I will ask you always,
PRAY FOR US NOW...

...and at the hour of our death. Amen!

And now I can say the whole prayer:

Hail Mary,
full of grace,
the Lord
is with you.
Blessed are you
among women,
and blessed is the fruit
of your womb, Jesus.
Holy Mary,
Mother of God,
pray for us
sinners,
now
and at the hour
of our death.

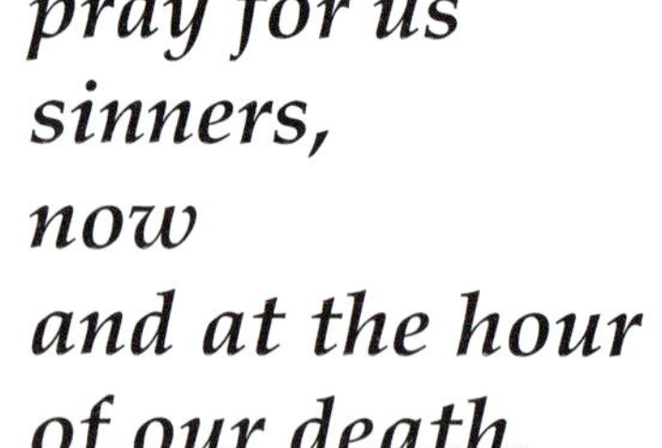

It is a beautiful prayer,
which says many things.
I am happy
that I learned it.
It is a prayer
which deserves to end with
a beautiful

Amen!

"Amen" means
"let it be like this,"
I agree,
Jesus.

BOOKS & MEDIA

CALIFORNIA
3908 Sepulveda Blvd., Culver City, CA 90230; 310-397-8676
5945 Balboa Ave., San Diego, CA 92111; 619-565-9181
46 Geary Street, San Francisco, CA 94108; 415-781-5180
FLORIDA
145 S.W. 107th Ave., Miami, FL 33174; 305-559-6715
HAWAII
1143 Bishop Street, Honolulu, HI 96813; 808-521-2731
ILLINOIS
172 North Michigan Ave., Chicago, IL 60601; 312-346-4228
LOUISIANA
4403 Veterans Memorial Blvd., Metairie, LA 70006; 504-887-7631
MASSACHUSETTS
50 St. Paul's Ave., Jamaica Plain, Boston, MA 02130; 617-522-8911
Rte. 1, 885 Providence Hwy., Dedham, MA 02026; 781-326-5385
MISSOURI
9804 Watson Rd., St. Louis, MO 63126; 314-965-3512
NEW JERSEY
561 U.S. Route 1, Wick Plaza, Edison, NJ 08817; 732-572-1200
NEW YORK
150 East 52nd Street, New York, NY 10022; 212-754-1110
78 Fort Place, Staten Island, NY 10301; 718-447-5071
OHIO
2105 Ontario Street (at Prospect Ave.), Cleveland, OH 44115; 216-621-9427
PENNSYLVANIA
9171-A Roosevelt Blvd., Philadelphia, PA 19114; 215-676-9494
SOUTH CAROLINA
243 King Street, Charleston, SC 29401; 803-577-0175
TENNESSEE
4811 Poplar Ave., Memphis, TN 38117 901-761-2987
TEXAS
114 Main Plaza, San Antonio, TX 78205; 210-224-8101
VIRGINIA
1025 King Street, Alexandria, VA 22314; 703-549-3806
CANADA
3022 Dufferin Street, Toronto, Ontario, Canada M6B 3T5; 416-781-9131
1155 Yonge Street, Toronto, Ontario, Canada M4T 1W2; 416-934-3440

Nihil Obstat:
Rev. Richard V. Lawlor, SJ
Imprimatur:
+Humberto Cardinal Medeiros
Archbishop of Boston

ISBN 0-8198-3316-9

Printed and published in the U.S.A. by Pauline Books & Media, 50 St. Paul's Avenue, Boston, MA 02130.

http://www.pauline.org

Pauline Books & Media is the publishing house of the Daughters of St. Paul, an international congregation of women religious serving the Church with the communications media.

4 5 6 7 8 9 10 03 02 01 00 99 98